The Final Days

Life Inside the White House

Arthur Crandon LL.B (Hons) M.A.

ISBN: 9798305121315

This book provides a compelling insider account of life in the White House, offering unique perspectives on the personal, political, and cultural dynamics that shape the lives of those who serve at the highest levels of government. Blending personal stories, behind-the-scenes anecdotes, and reflections on historical moments of a fictional transition, the book would appeal to readers fascinated by politics, leadership, and the untold stories of power.

CONTENTS

PROLOGUE: THE CLOCK IS TICKING

David Kincaid stood in the center of the oval office, the early morning light streaming through the tall windows behind him. The soft hum of Washington stirred outside as the city awakened to another day. His gaze locked onto the Washington monument, standing tall and unyielding against the horizon, a symbol of endurance. But endurance, Kincaid thought wryly, was easier for stone and marble than for flesh and blood.

The countdown had begun. Six months remained until the new administration would take over, and his term would be reduced to history. What kind of history, though? That was the question gnawing at him.

Reflections on legacy

Kincaid turned, his eyes settling on the resolute desk. The desk had borne the weight of decisions that changed the course of nations, yet in its stoic silence, it seemed to mock him now. There were victories he was proud of—the healthcare reforms that had brought coverage to millions, the diplomatic accord that had averted war in the pacific—but there were also failures. His inability to push through the sweeping climate initiative haunted him. Time, he realized, was no longer an ally.

On the desk lay a leather-bound briefing book, thick with reports, memos, and action items. His chief of staff, Claire Rivers, had scribbled on the cover in her no-nonsense handwriting: *"legacy priority agenda: 6 months."* The term "legacy" seemed almost ironic in the face of recent developments. A persistent leak from within his administration had raised questions about national security. The press, always hungry for blood, speculated endlessly about who was responsible.

The weight of scandal

Kincaid's fingers tightened around the edge of the desk. The scandal could undo everything. For weeks, classified information had trickled out to the media, details about covert operations and private meetings that should never have seen the light of day. A whistleblower? A traitor? Or just incompetence? The answer remained elusive, and the uncertainty festered.

The previous night, his national security advisor, Tom Anders, had presented a grim update. "it's someone close, Mr. President. Someone in the west wing," Anders had said, his voice low but firm. The words lingered like a dark cloud, eclipsing even the dawn light pouring into the room now.

Unresolved battles

The scandal wasn't the only weight pressing on Kincaid. Across the hall, in the Roosevelt room, Claire was likely preparing the morning's agenda. On it would be the climate treaty, a signature policy initiative he'd fought for throughout his presidency. It remained stalled in congress, blocked by partisan gridlock and opposition from industries afraid of losing their bottom lines.
Claire's insistence echoed in his mind: *"you can still get this through. One last win. The one people will remember."* She believed in his ability to rally the nation, to twist arms on capitol hill. But Kincaid wasn't sure if he believed it himself anymore.

Personal tensions

His thoughts drifted to Caroline, his daughter, whose recent moves had brought fresh tension to an already strained family dynamic. She had hinted at writing a memoir—a tell-all that would expose the sacrifices, the compromises, and the private cracks in their public facade. He had tried to talk her out of it, but the conversation had devolved into a shouting match, with Caroline accusing him of caring more about his image than his family.

He sighed, the sound heavy with frustration. The presidency had cost him more than he'd ever anticipated. And yet, here he was, clinging to the last threads of power, desperate to make them count.

Setting the tone

Outside, the press corps buzzed like bees around the hive. Camera crews adjusted their angles as reporters speculated about the agenda for the president's morning briefing. A phrase floated through the airwaves, cutting into the room's quiet: *"lame duck."*

Kincaid's jaw tightened. *Lame duck.* The term carried a sting, a cruel reminder of his waning influence. Yet, the clock ticking down didn't signal the end for him—it Signaled urgency. There was still time, however fleeting, to define how history would remember David Kincaid.

A glimpse of what's to come

Behind the door, footsteps echoed—Claire's sharp heels clicking against the marble floor. She entered briskly, a file in her hand and determination in her eyes. "Mr. President, the briefing is in ten minutes. We need to address the leaks today."

He turned toward her, the resolve hardening in his

gaze. "we'll address it. But first, I want to talk about the treaty. If we're going down, Claire, we're going down swinging."

The tension in the room hung thick, but beneath it was something else—a spark. Kincaid was not done fighting. As the door closed behind them, the clock on the wall ticked steadily, each second marking the approach of an ending—but also, perhaps, a beginning.

1 THE LAST CAMPAIGN

President David Kincaid stood at the head of the Oval Office table, the morning's light casting sharp shadows across the faces of his senior advisors. The tension in the room was palpable. Before him lay a draft of the climate treaty—a culmination of years of negotiation and compromise, now hanging by a thread. This treaty could define his legacy, yet the resistance was coming from the unlikeliest place: his own party.

The Pressure to Act

Claire Rivers, his razor-sharp Chief of Staff, leaned forward, her voice cutting through the room like steel. "Mr. President, if we don't move now, this treaty dies. We have a slim window to push this through Congress before the opposition rallies more support."

Her words hung in the air, but the President's brow furrowed. The polls told a grim story. His approval ratings had dipped below 40%, with critics labeling him as ineffective in his final months. The media had dubbed the climate treaty a "Hail Mary," a desperate attempt to salvage his presidency. Kincaid knew the stakes—but so did his detractors.

Internal Conflict

Senator Evelyn Monroe, a key figure in his party's moderate faction, had publicly voiced concerns that the treaty would alienate critical industries, particularly coal and manufacturing. "We're looking at a jobs crisis in swing states, Mr. President," she'd said in a recent meeting. "We can't afford to lose them over this."

Privately, Monroe's objections carried another weight. She had allies who were already aligning themselves with Vice President Robert Sinclair, who had been noticeably absent from recent climate policy discussions.

The Vice President's Hidden Agenda

Unbeknownst to Kincaid, Sinclair had begun quietly meeting with key lobbyists and party donors. He was laying the groundwork for his own presidential bid, positioning himself as a voice of moderation in contrast to Kincaid's "idealism."

Sinclair's strategy was simple: let the treaty fail. A high-profile defeat would weaken Kincaid's standing, making it easier for Sinclair to step into the spotlight as a pragmatic leader capable of bridging divides.

The Oval Office Debate

The scene was set for confrontation. Kincaid called a closed-door meeting with his senior staff, key advisors, and Sinclair to finalize the strategy for the treaty's passage.

Claire began the meeting with her usual precision. "The treaty is achievable, but we need to neutralize Monroe and secure the coalition. We're short five votes, but I believe we can turn at least three with the right incentives."

Sinclair leaned back in his chair, arms crossed. His expression was measured but subtly dismissive. "And the other two? Even if we scrape by, this bill could backfire. The industries we're alienating fund half of our campaign infrastructure. I think it's worth considering whether this is the right time to push a treaty this ambitious."

The room froze. Kincaid's eyes narrowed, his voice cutting like a blade. "Are you suggesting we abandon this? After everything we've worked for?"

Sinclair didn't flinch. "I'm suggesting we focus on what's realistic, David. This treaty is symbolic, but at what cost? Jobs? Elections? The party's future?"

The air was thick with unspoken accusations. Claire shot Sinclair a glare that could have frozen the Potomac. "Realistic? The right time? Mr. Vice President, if we keep waiting for the 'right time,' nothing will ever change."

Kincaid slammed his fist on the Resolute Desk, the sharp crack reverberating through the room. "Enough! Loyalty, Sinclair. Loyalty to the people who elected us to lead—not to the donors, not to the party machine."

His voice softened, but the anger in his eyes remained. "This isn't about my legacy. This is about the world we leave behind. I didn't come this far to back down now."

The Fallout

As the meeting adjourned, Claire pulled Kincaid aside. "He's not on our side," she said bluntly.

Kincaid sighed, running a hand through his hair. "I know. But we don't have time to fight on two fronts. Keep him close—for now."

Meanwhile, Sinclair left the room and immediately texted an ally: *"He's doubling down on the treaty. We may need to speed things up."*

2 SHADOWS IN THE WEST WING

The soft hum of fluorescent lights filled the silence of the West Wing that evening, the atmosphere thick with tension. President David Kincaid sat at his desk, his fingers drumming against the polished wood of the Resolute Desk. In his hands was a classified briefing—no longer classified, thanks to a leak that had blindsided the administration and sent ripples through the halls of power. Somewhere, someone in this very building had betrayed him, and the consequences were unraveling faster than they could contain.

The Leak Emerges

That morning, *The Sentinel*, a major news outlet, had broken a bombshell story exposing a covert U.S. intelligence operation aimed at dismantling cyber-attacks emanating from Eastern Europe. The operation wasn't just secret—it was vital, a cornerstone of U.S. strategy in a volatile region. The article, rich with detail, revealed codenames, deployment strategies, and even fragments of internal discussions.

By the time Kincaid read it, the damage was already spreading. Calls flooded in from allied leaders, each questioning the U.S.'s ability to safeguard sensitive information. The Pentagon demanded answers. The media swarmed with speculation, circling the administration like vultures.

Tom Anders, Kincaid's unflappable National Security Advisor, had been the first to brief him. "This wasn't an accident," Anders said, laying a folder on the desk. "Someone inside knew exactly what they were doing. They didn't just leak—they targeted."

"Targeted?" Kincaid's voice was steady but sharp.

"They released enough to expose the operation but held back just enough to sow doubt about our internal security. This wasn't just about the information—it was about undermining trust."

A Breach of Trust

Trust. It was the currency of the West Wing, and now it was bleeding out. Allegations swirled as staffers eyed one another with suspicion. Meetings became guarded, every word weighed carefully. Claire Rivers, Kincaid's razor-sharp Chief of Staff, quickly stepped in to try to contain the chaos.

"I want every department's communications audited," she ordered during a tense strategy session in her office. "Nobody's above scrutiny—not the interns, not the senior advisors, not even me."

But her decisiveness couldn't stem the whispers. Some pointed fingers at the Vice President's office, citing Robert Sinclair's recent diplomatic trip to Eastern Europe. Others hinted at a disgruntled policy advisor who had clashed with Kincaid over recent decisions.

Sinclair, always poised, played his part well. "It's critical we get to the bottom of this," he told Kincaid during a one-on-one meeting. "The country needs to see strength right now. But we should be careful about jumping to conclusions."

Something in his tone made Kincaid pause. Was it genuine concern—or calculated deflection?

Megan Carter's Discovery

As the administration scrambled for answers, Megan Carter, a junior aide in the communications office, worked late into the night in the cramped confines of her cubicle. Her task was mundane: comb through flagged emails for anything unusual. Most were routine—briefing drafts, scheduling notes—but one thread stopped her cold.

The email chain was encrypted, its sender listed as "Anonymous." Megan's hands trembled as she opened it. The messages referenced the leaked operation in chillingly precise detail, alongside terms like "leverage" and "exposure." One email included a forwarded message from a foreign diplomat, thinly veiled in diplomatic language but unmistakably gloating over the fallout.

Megan's stomach churned. She knew enough to recognize the gravity of what she'd found. But she also knew the risks. Who could she trust? With a deep breath, she forwarded the emails to Tom Anders, marking them URGENT. Then she packed her bag and left, feeling the eyes of an unseen watcher as she walked out of the building.

The Situation Room Revelation

By midnight, Kincaid was back in the Situation Room, flanked by Anders, Rivers, and a handful of top security officials. The room's dim lighting and the hum of monitors gave the meeting a conspiratorial air.

Anders stood at the head of the table, the emails Megan had uncovered displayed on a screen. "These messages were sent from within the West Wing," he began. "And they were routed through a private server linked to one of our closest allies."

Kincaid leaned forward, his voice low and deliberate. "Which ally?"

Anders hesitated before answering. "The United Kingdom. Specifically, a diplomatic office with direct ties to Vice President Sinclair's Eastern European trip last month."

The room fell silent. Claire was the first to break it. "You're suggesting Sinclair's involved?"

"I'm not suggesting anything," Anders replied, his tone measured. "But the timing, the access— none of it looks good."

Kincaid's jaw tightened. "Until we have undeniable proof, this stays within this room. I won't have a public witch hunt. But Tom, I want you to dig deeper. If Sinclair's behind this..." His voice trailed off, the unspoken consequences heavy in the air.

Megan's Danger

As the meeting adjourned, Megan's phone

buzzed with an anonymous message: *"You've seen enough. Drop it, or there will be consequences."*

Her heart pounded. Someone knew. She glanced around her darkened apartment, the silence pressing in like a weight. For the first time, she realized the enormity of what she had stumbled into—and the danger it brought.

3 THE FIRST FAMILY'S STRUGGLES

The long dining table in the private quarters of the White House stretched between them, more a symbol of distance than connection. Caroline Kincaid, the 26-year-old first daughter, sat at one end, arms crossed, her plate barely touched. Her father, President David Kincaid, sat at the other, his tie loosened but his expression stern. The air between them was tense, heavy with years of unspoken frustrations that were now threatening to erupt.

Caroline's Turmoil

Caroline had never wanted the spotlight. Her life, once relatively private despite her father's political career, had been thrust into the relentless glare of media attention when Kincaid took office. Every misstep, every comment, every relationship had become fodder for the tabloids.

Her social media had been combed through, her college friendships scrutinized. Even her decision to take a break from law school had been painted as an act of rebellion. But the final straw was the latest article in *Capital Chronicle*, which accused her of being a liability to her father's administration, citing her "reckless behavior" and "inability to align with the President's image."

Now, as whispers about her writing a memoir began circulating, the tension between Caroline and her father had reached its boiling point.

The Dinner Scene: Fractured Bonds

"Caroline, I need to talk to you about this book." Kincaid's voice was calm, too calm, a practiced tone that only made her bristle more.

"It's not a book," Caroline snapped, her fork clattering against her plate as she dropped it. "It's my story. And for once, I'd like to have control over something in my life."

Kincaid leaned forward, his hands resting on

the table. "Your story is tied to this family, Caroline. To this administration. Do you have any idea what kind of damage this could do? We're six months away from leaving this office—do you really want to add fuel to the fire now?"

Caroline's eyes flashed with anger. "This isn't about damage control, Dad. This is about me. About the years I've spent being paraded around like some perfect accessory to your legacy while you ignored what it's cost me."

"That's not fair," Kincaid shot back, his calm veneer cracking. "I've done everything I could to protect you and your mother from this life."

"Protect us?" Caroline's voice rose, trembling with a mix of hurt and rage. "You didn't protect us—you used us. Mom had to smile through every campaign rally while you made promises that kept her up at night. And me? I was shoved into a role I never asked for, expected to just...be okay with it."

"You think I wanted this for you?" Kincaid's fist hit the table, the sound echoing in the room. "You think I don't regret the sacrifices we've all had to make? But I had a responsibility to this country— to the people who trusted me to lead."

"And what about your responsibility to us?" Caroline's voice cracked, her eyes glistening with unshed tears. "Or does that only matter when the cameras are rolling?"

The room fell silent, the weight of her words

hanging between them. Outside, the muffled sound of reporters gathering near the gates of the White House seeped into the room, a reminder that their lives were never truly private.

A Public Reminder of Private Struggles

Unable to stay any longer, Caroline shoved back her chair and stormed out, her heels clicking sharply against the marble floor. Kincaid called after her, but she didn't stop. She made her way down the hall, brushing past an aide who looked too stunned to speak.

As she exited through the side door, a small group of reporters caught sight of her. Flashes went off like lightning, their cameras capturing her tear-streaked face as she hurried to her waiting car. "Caroline! Caroline! Any comment on the book rumors?" one of them shouted.

She ignored them, her mind racing. She hadn't even decided if she would write the memoir, but in that moment, the idea felt less like an option and more like a necessity—a way to reclaim her voice in a world that had silenced her for too long.

Kincaid's Reflection

Back in the dining room, Kincaid sat alone, the weight of their argument pressing down on him. He stared at her untouched plate and thought of the little girl she had once been, the one who used to climb into his lap and insist on "helping" him with his speeches by doodling on his notes.

How had they ended up here? Was it inevitable, or had he truly failed her? He thought of the sacrifices he had made for the presidency, the nights spent away from his family, the moments he could never get back.

Claire Rivers found him there an hour later, the room dark save for the dim light over the table. "Mr. President?" she asked gently.

He didn't look up. "How do you protect the people you love," he said softly, "when the job demands so much of you?"

Claire hesitated before answering. "Sometimes you can't," she admitted. "But what matters is that you try."

4 THE HIDDEN AGENDA

The West Wing was quieter than usual, the kind of quiet that amplifies unease. President Kincaid sat in his private study, the soft glow of a desk lamp illuminating the intelligence briefing in his hands. The words on the page confirmed what he had feared but hoped wasn't true: a senior member of his administration had been working with a powerful corporate lobby to sabotage the climate treaty—the signature policy of his presidency. The betrayal cut deeper than he expected, and the implications extended far beyond the treaty itself.

The Revelation

The report had come from Tom Anders, who had followed a suspicious trail of emails and undisclosed meetings. The culprit was Michael Harrington, Deputy Chief of Policy, someone Kincaid had trusted for years. Harrington had been covertly feeding inside information about the treaty's weaknesses to a corporate lobbying group representing fossil fuel interests. Their goal was clear: derail the treaty before it could pass Congress and solidify a regulatory framework that would impact their bottom line for decades.

"This isn't just lobbying," Anders had said earlier that day in a private meeting. "They've been leveraging this information to pressure key senators. Harrington is essentially giving them a roadmap to kill the bill."

Kincaid's jaw tightened as he reread the report. Harrington had always been pragmatic, someone who played the game of politics with calculated precision. But this wasn't pragmatism—it was betrayal. And worse, it wasn't just about policy. Anders' report hinted at something deeper, a personal vendetta that might have fueled Harrington's actions.

Conflict Within the Administration

Later that evening, Kincaid summoned Claire

Rivers to his office. Her expression darkened as he handed her the briefing. She scanned it quickly, her lips pressing into a thin line as she read.

"Harrington," she muttered. "Of course."

"You're not surprised?" Kincaid asked, watching her carefully.

"Surprised he'd stoop this low? No. Surprised he managed to keep it quiet this long? A little." She sat down, her voice tight with restrained anger. "Michael Harrington has always been more loyal to his ambitions than to this administration. But this—this is different."

Kincaid leaned forward. "Why?"

Claire hesitated, then met his gaze. "It's personal. Years ago, I blocked him from a promotion at the State Department. He wasn't qualified, and I made it clear. He's resented me ever since."

"So this isn't just about the treaty," Kincaid said slowly. "It's about taking you down, too."

"Seems like a two-for-one deal," Claire said bitterly.

The President's Dilemma

Kincaid faced a difficult choice. Confronting Harrington directly could expose the betrayal, but it also risked triggering a public scandal that would weaken his administration in its final months. Using the information strategically, however, could allow him to neutralize the threat quietly—perhaps even turn it to his advantage.

"We need to tread carefully," Claire said, her tone measured. "If this goes public, it'll give the opposition exactly what they need to discredit the treaty—and us."

"But letting him stay gives him more time to sabotage us," Kincaid countered. "I'm not willing to sit by while he works against everything we've built."

Claire nodded. "Then we make sure he doesn't have the chance."

The Rose Garden Meeting

Late that night, under the cover of darkness, Kincaid met Anders and Claire in the Rose Garden. The location was deliberate—no cameras, no prying eyes, just the soft rustle of leaves and the distant hum of Washington.

Anders laid out the full scope of Harrington's activities, including details of meetings with corporate executives and leaked strategy documents. "They've got senators in their pocket," Anders said. "If this leaks, it'll look like your administration is riddled with corruption."

Claire folded her arms, her jaw tight. "And if we do nothing, Harrington hands them the win."

Kincaid paced, his hands clasped behind his back. The betrayal stung deeply, but he couldn't let emotion cloud his judgment. "What are our options?"

"We could confront him privately," Anders suggested. "Force his resignation and spin it as a personal decision. Quiet, controlled."

Claire shook her head. "No. He doesn't deserve a clean exit. If we let him go quietly, he'll take that as a win and walk straight into a lucrative job with these lobbyists."

Kincaid stopped pacing. "Then we box him in. We leak just enough to put the lobbyists under scrutiny. Force them to distance themselves from him, and make it clear we know exactly what he's been up to."

"And Harrington?" Claire asked.

Kincaid's expression hardened. "We let him twist. He'll know we're watching his every move. He won't dare step out of line."

The Personal Stakes

As the meeting ended, Claire lingered behind with Kincaid. "This isn't just about Harrington," she said quietly. "It's about everything we've fought for. If we let this slip, it'll define your presidency."

"I know," Kincaid said, his voice heavy. "But it's more than that. It's about trust. If people like Harrington can do this under my watch, what does that say about me?"

"It says you trusted the wrong person," Claire replied. "But it also says you're willing to fight for the right ones."

Themes Explored
1. Trust and Betrayal: Harrington's actions highlight the fragility of loyalty in politics and the personal cost of betrayal.
2. Moral Dilemmas: Kincaid's decision reflects the complexity of leadership—balancing justice with pragmatism in the face of adversity.
3. Personal Stakes: Claire's history with Harrington adds emotional depth, turning the conflict into more than just a political battle.

5 THE PARDONS LIST

The weight of legacy hung heavy in the Oval Office as President David Kincaid stared at the thick folder on the coffee table before him. Marked *Confidential*, the document was an annual ritual for every outgoing president: the list of pardon requests. But this year's list wasn't just controversial—it was a minefield. Among the names was one that threatened to overshadow his final months in office: Richard Hayes, his former Secretary of Commerce, disgraced and facing trial for corruption.

The Background

Richard Hayes had been a rising star in Kincaid's administration—a charismatic dealmaker with an enviable track record in trade negotiations. But his fall from grace had been swift and public. Leaked documents revealed that Hayes had accepted bribes from foreign entities in exchange for favorable trade policies, a scandal that rocked the administration and forced his resignation.

Now, facing a likely conviction, Hayes had submitted a formal request for a presidential pardon. The legal team's argument was simple: a pardon would keep Hayes from testifying, potentially shielding the administration from further scrutiny. But granting it would ignite public outrage and cement the perception that Kincaid's White House prioritized loyalty over accountability.

The Oval Office Discussion

The room was tense as Kincaid's inner circle gathered. Claire Rivers stood by the fireplace, arms crossed, her expression a mix of frustration and determination. Tom Anders sat to her right, flipping through the list, while Kincaid leaned forward in his chair, his fingers steepled under his chin.

"We can't ignore the optics, Mr. President," said Peter Walsh, the White House Counsel. "Hayes's trial could drag this administration through the mud. Every headline will tie him back to you."

"And pardoning him will look worse," Claire countered sharply. "It'll scream 'cover-up.' The press will crucify us, and the public will see it as a betrayal of the accountability you promised when you took office."

Walsh adjusted his glasses. "There's a middle ground here. We can frame it as an act of compassion—a recognition of his service, not an exoneration of his mistakes."

Kincaid slammed his hand on the arm of the chair. "Compassion? For a man who sold out this country to line his pockets? No. I didn't work this hard to let my presidency end in shame."

Personal Stakes

As the debate raged, Kincaid felt the familiar pull of conflicting loyalties. Hayes had been a friend—a close ally in the administration's early years. They had shared late-night strategy sessions and celebratory toasts after successful trade deals. But the betrayal had cut deep, and Kincaid wasn't sure if he could separate the personal from the political.

Claire's voice broke through his thoughts. "David, if you do this, you're not just protecting

Hayes—you're protecting every corrupt politician who thinks they can buy their way out of accountability. You're better than this."

Kincaid's gaze shifted to Anders. "Tom, where do you stand?"

Anders hesitated, then spoke carefully. "The risks of not pardoning him are real. Hayes knows things—damaging things. If he testifies, it could open doors we've kept closed."

"But is that worth compromising everything we stand for?" Kincaid asked, his voice heavy with exhaustion.

The Climax: A Defining Moment

The discussion reached its peak when Walsh pushed a folder across the table. "Mr. President, it's not just about Hayes. Look at the other names. Low-level offenders. People who deserve a second chance. If we don't act now, their lives stay ruined. Hayes can be part of a broader list. He'll get lost in the noise."

Kincaid opened the folder, flipping through the names. A mother of three convicted for drug possession. A whistleblower jailed for exposing corporate fraud. Veterans serving time for nonviolent offenses. Each name was a story, a plea for redemption.

Then his eyes fell on Hayes's name, bold and unapologetic. His gut tightened. He closed the folder with a snap.

"No," he said firmly, rising to his feet. "I won't let this become another political transaction. Every person on that list has earned their pardon—except him."

Walsh opened his mouth to protest, but Kincaid cut him off. "I've made my decision. Hayes gets nothing."

Reaching down, he tore Hayes's request from the folder, ripping it clean in half. "I won't let my presidency end in shame."

The Fallout

As the meeting dispersed, Claire lingered behind. "That was the right call," she said softly.

Kincaid exhaled deeply, sinking back into his chair. "Then why does it feel like I've just made another enemy?"

"Because you probably have," Claire admitted. "But enemies don't define legacies. Principles do."

6 A FOREIGN CRISIS

The breaking news alert scrolled across every major network as President David Kincaid sat in the Situation Room, his cabinet gathered around the long mahogany table. The headline read: *Ally's Government Toppled Amid Protests; U.S. Embassy Besieged.* The images accompanying the story were worse: mobs surrounding the U.S. Embassy, their chants audible even through the thick security gates. Flames from a nearby vehicle cast shadows on the building's facade as embassy staff huddled inside, awaiting orders.

This was not how Kincaid had envisioned the final months of his presidency. He was supposed to be wrapping up his tenure, ensuring a smooth transition, and solidifying his legacy. Instead, he faced a crisis that could escalate into bloodshed—or worse, war.

The Crisis Unfolds

The crisis began three days earlier in Larniva, a fictional Eastern European nation known for its strategic alliances with NATO and the United States. A simmering economic downturn, coupled with corruption scandals, had sparked protests against President Nikolai Vaskov, a close ally of Kincaid's administration. By morning, Vaskov had fled the capital, leaving a power vacuum that plunged Larniva into chaos.

Protesters viewed the U.S. Embassy as a symbol of their government's corruption, accusing it of propping up Vaskov's regime. Demonstrations turned violent, and the embassy's security team was quickly overwhelmed. Inside, a mix of diplomats, Marine guards, and local staff awaited instructions as their situation grew increasingly precarious.

The Situation Room Debate

In the Situation Room, voices clashed as Kincaid's advisors debated the next steps.

General Alan Weaver, the Joint Chiefs' representative, leaned forward, his voice measured but firm. "Mr. President, we need to mobilize forces. A rapid deployment team can secure the embassy and extract personnel if necessary. Time is critical—if the compound is breached, we risk a diplomatic catastrophe."

Across the table, Angela Perez, Kincaid's senior political advisor, shook her head. "Deploying troops in your final months? That's political suicide, sir. The optics alone—sending soldiers into a collapsing nation—will overshadow everything you've accomplished. This could define your legacy."

"And if we do nothing?" Weaver countered. "We let Americans die on foreign soil? You think that won't define his legacy?"

Claire Rivers, seated beside Kincaid, raised her hand for silence. "There's a middle ground. We coordinate with NATO allies, share the burden. This isn't just our crisis—it's theirs too."

Kincaid finally spoke, his voice calm but commanding. "What's the status on the ground?"

A Call to the Front Line

Moments later, a screen flickered to life, connecting Kincaid to Captain Ryan Hale, the Marine officer in charge at the embassy. Hale's face was streaked with sweat and soot, the sound of distant shouting audible through his headset.

"Mr. President," Hale began, his voice steady despite the chaos behind him. "We've secured the staff in the safe room, but the perimeter is failing. The crowd's growing, and we've got reports of armed agitators in the mix. We need direction, sir."

Kincaid's jaw tightened. "What are your options, Captain?"

Hale hesitated. "We can hold for now, but if the crowd breaches the gate, we'll lose control fast. Extraction is risky without reinforcements."

"And the local security forces?"

"They've pulled back, sir. The city's in freefall."

Kincaid's silence stretched for a moment, the weight of the decision pressing down on him. Finally, he said, "Captain, hold your position. Reinforcements are being mobilized."

The Tipping Point

After the call, Kincaid turned back to his team. "We're not abandoning our people. Get the NATO partners on the line. If we go in, we're not going alone."

The hours that followed were a blur of tense negotiations. France agreed to deploy a contingent of peacekeepers, while Germany committed logistical support. Still, the onus fell on the U.S. to lead the operation.

As the reinforcements mobilized, protests outside the embassy escalated. A Molotov cocktail struck the compound's outer wall, and the sound of gunfire crackled in the distance. Inside, Captain Hale relayed updates, his calm demeanor steadying his team as they prepared for evacuation.

The Decision to Evacuate

By midnight, the reinforcements had arrived. Kincaid made the final call: a coordinated evacuation under the cover of darkness. Helicopters swooped in, and a convoy of armored vehicles ferried embassy staff to safety.

As the operation unfolded, Kincaid remained in the Situation Room, monitoring every detail. When the final helicopter lifted off, he allowed himself a brief moment of relief. But the cost of the crisis lingered in his mind.

The Fallout

The next morning, headlines were as divided as his advisors had predicted. *President Kincaid Mobilizes Troops in Diplomatic Rescue* read one. Another declared, *Larniva Crisis Exposes Weakness of U.S. Foreign Policy.*

In a private meeting later that day, Claire approached him. "You made the right call, David. You put people above politics."

"But will anyone see it that way?" he asked, his voice heavy with exhaustion.

"They will," she said firmly. "Maybe not today, but they will."

7 THE SUCCESSOR'S SHADOW

The buzz around President-elect Linda Monroe began long before her inauguration. Her dynamic transition team, a well-oiled machine of media-savvy strategists and policy experts, was already dominating headlines. Every announcement about her bold agenda—centering on economic growth and deregulation—seemed calculated to eclipse President Kincaid's final months. For Kincaid, the shadow of her incoming administration wasn't just an annoyance—it was a direct threat to the legacy he had worked so hard to build.

The Rising Tensions

Monroe had run her campaign as a centrist reformer, pledging to "clean house" and return government to "practical, people-first policies." Her platform had appealed to moderates and independents disillusioned by partisanship, but her rhetoric often dismissed Kincaid's policies as overly idealistic and ineffective.

Now, as her team leaked plans to reverse several of his key initiatives—most notably the climate treaty—Kincaid found himself not just sidelined but actively undermined.

A particularly pointed article in *The Capitol Times* read: *"Monroe's team quietly signals a shift away from the Kincaid-era climate agenda, citing concerns over economic impact."* The piece, citing unnamed sources, implied that Monroe's administration would focus on industry partnerships rather than sweeping regulations—a move that many saw as pandering to powerful corporate interests.

The Private Meeting

Determined to address the brewing conflict directly, Kincaid invited Monroe to the White House for a private meeting. The meeting, billed as a cordial transition discussion, quickly devolved into a tense exchange behind closed doors.

Scene: The Oval Office Showdown

Linda Monroe entered the Oval Office with her trademark confidence, her sharp navy pantsuit as unyielding as her handshake. Kincaid motioned for her to sit, his expression calm but unreadable.

"Linda," he began, "thank you for making the time. I thought it was important we had a frank discussion about the climate treaty."

She offered a polite smile. "Of course, David. What's on your mind?"

Kincaid leaned forward, his hands clasped. "I've seen the reports. Your team's been signaling a rollback on the treaty. I need to know—are you planning to abandon it?"

Monroe's smile tightened. "I wouldn't say abandon. But we're re-evaluating its economic impact. There's a lot of concern from industry leaders—manufacturing, energy. They feel the current framework is too restrictive."

"And what about the long-term impact?" Kincaid countered, his tone sharpening. "This treaty isn't just a policy—it's a statement. It's leadership. If we back away now, we're signaling to the world that we don't take climate change seriously."

Monroe held his gaze, unflinching. "With respect, David, I ran on a platform of balance. People are struggling to pay their bills. They're worried about their jobs—not about hitting arbitrary climate targets."

Kincaid's voice rose slightly. "Arbitrary? You think the rising seas, the wildfires, the droughts are arbitrary? This treaty is the culmination of years of work—work that's already brought major players to the table. Do you know how hard it was to get China and India to agree to emissions caps? You pull out now, and that progress evaporates."

Monroe's tone remained measured, but there was a steeliness beneath it. "I respect the work you've done, David, but I was elected to make my own decisions. My team and I will do what's best for the country, even if that means taking a different direction."

Kincaid stood, the weight of his frustration palpable. "Linda, I'm not asking you to agree with everything I've done. I'm asking you to consider the bigger picture. The world is watching."

She stood as well, her polite mask slipping just slightly. "And so are the American people. They're watching for leadership that works for them—not for global applause."

For a moment, neither spoke, the unspoken tension crackling between them. Finally, Monroe broke the silence. "I appreciate your passion, David. I really do. But this is my administration now. And I have to do what I believe is right."

Kincaid's Frustration

As Monroe left, Kincaid remained standing by the Resolute Desk, his hands pressed against its surface. He stared out the window at the South Lawn, feeling the weight of inevitability. The meeting had confirmed what he already suspected: Monroe had no intention of championing the climate treaty.

"Damn it," he muttered under his breath. It wasn't just about the treaty—it was about everything. The erosion of his policies, the slow dismantling of his vision. How much of his presidency would survive her administration?

Fallout and Intrigue

- The Media's Spin:

Hours after their meeting, anonymous leaks suggested that Monroe had firmly decided to reverse the climate treaty. Headlines speculated about a brewing feud between the outgoing and incoming administrations.

- Internal Discontent:

Claire Rivers, Kincaid's Chief of Staff, was livid. "She's undermining you before you're even out the door," she snapped during a late-night strategy session. "This isn't a transition—it's a takeover."

- Monroe's Calculations:

Monroe's team saw the treaty as low-hanging fruit—an easy way to distance herself from Kincaid while appealing to powerful industry players and centrist voters.

8 THE SCANDAL BREAKS

The news broke at dawn, sending shockwaves through the political landscape. The headline on every network and newsfeed was the same: *"West Wing Mole Unmasked: Scandal Rocks Kincaid Administration."* By mid-morning, it was the only topic dominating Washington.

The mole, Michael Harrington—the Deputy Chief of Policy—had been uncovered by the National Security Advisor, Tom Anders, who had been quietly tracking his movements for weeks. But Harrington wasn't working alone. His actions implicated other senior officials, exposing a web of leaks and unethical behavior that threatened to dismantle President Kincaid's already fragile administration.

The Unraveling

The revelation that Harrington had been leaking classified information and collaborating with powerful lobbyists sent the West Wing into chaos. Staffers whispered in hushed tones as a flurry of meetings erupted behind closed doors. The tension was palpable, an air of distrust settling over the White House like a storm cloud.

Tom Anders briefed Kincaid in the Oval Office. "Harrington's been feeding insider information to the lobbyists for months," he said, his voice calm but grave. "But the fallout doesn't stop with him. He's named others—three senior advisors and two department heads."

Kincaid leaned back in his chair, his jaw tightening. "How credible is his information?"

"Solid. He provided emails, recordings—enough to corroborate everything. If we don't act, the press will crucify us. But firing this many people, this high up? It'll make the administration look like it's falling apart."

Kincaid exhaled slowly, the weight of the decision pressing down on him. "It's already falling apart, Tom. The question is whether we can salvage it."

Conflict in the Inner Circle

Kincaid convened a meeting with his senior staff. Claire Rivers, ever the realist, didn't mince words. "We have to cut them loose. If we don't, this becomes your scandal, David. You'll look complicit."

Angela Perez, the communications director, disagreed. "And if we fire half the senior staff, we're admitting chaos in the administration. The press will frame it as a collapse."

"We're damned if we do, damned if we don't," Claire shot back. "But at least firing them shows you're taking responsibility."

Kincaid listened silently, his hands clasped on the table. Finally, he spoke. "What's the public narrative here? If we take action, how do we frame it?"

Angela hesitated, then said, "You emphasize integrity. You say you won't tolerate betrayal, no matter who it is. Make it about leadership. Make it about the people."

The Press Conference: A Defining Moment

The East Room was packed with reporters. The air buzzed with anticipation as Kincaid stepped up to the podium. Cameras flashed, and the room fell silent.

"Good morning," he began, his tone calm but

firm. "As many of you are aware, this morning my administration uncovered a breach of trust at the highest levels of government. A senior member of my staff, along with several others, engaged in actions that betrayed the trust of this administration and the American people."

His words were measured, each one landing with precision. "Let me be clear: I will not tolerate betrayal. Those implicated in this investigation have been relieved of their duties, effective immediately. While it is deeply painful to take this action, it is necessary to uphold the values this administration stands for—integrity, accountability, and service to the American people."

The reporters erupted with questions. "Mr. President, do you take responsibility for allowing this to happen under your watch?" one shouted.

Kincaid met the reporter's gaze. "The buck always stops with me," he said. "And as President, I accept that responsibility. But leadership is not about avoiding mistakes—it's about how you respond when they happen. Today, I am taking decisive action to ensure this administration remains focused on its mission."

Another reporter pressed, "How can the American people trust your administration moving forward?"

Kincaid paused, the weight of the moment evident. "Trust is not given—it's earned. And I intend to spend every remaining day of my presidency earning that trust back."

The room was silent for a moment before the barrage of questions resumed. Kincaid held up a hand. "That's all for now," he said, stepping away from the podium. The flash of cameras followed him as he exited the room, his expression resolute.

The Fallout

Back in the Oval Office, Claire entered quietly, closing the door behind her. "That was a good speech," she said.

Kincaid sat behind the Resolute Desk, his shoulders slumped slightly. "Was it enough?"

"It's never enough," Claire admitted. "But it was honest. And that matters."

Kincaid nodded, staring out the window. The reporters were still camped on the lawn, their lenses trained on the building. "I didn't come this far to let it end like this," he said quietly.

"Then don't," Claire replied. "The next move is yours."

9 THE FAREWELL ADDRESS

The hours leading up to President David Kincaid's farewell address were filled with a quiet intensity. The speech, which would be broadcast live to millions, was not just an opportunity to reflect—it was his last chance to frame his legacy on his terms. But as he sat alone in the family residence, reviewing his handwritten notes, the words felt insufficient. How could he distill the triumphs, failures, and lessons of his presidency into a single moment?

The weight of the office, which had felt so heavy in the past few months, seemed to press down on him even harder now. Yet, what occupied his mind most was not the speech, but the strained relationship with his daughter, Caroline

A Quiet Moment with Caroline

Kincaid looked up as the door to the residence creaked open. Caroline stepped inside hesitantly, her arms crossed defensively. "Mom said I should come talk to you," she said, her voice soft but laced with tension.

"Caroline," Kincaid began, setting the notes aside. "I'm glad you're here. I've been meaning to—"

"To apologize?" she interrupted, her eyebrow raised. "For putting this family through hell for the last eight years?"

He winced but nodded. "Yes. For that, and for everything else."

Caroline crossed the room and sat down across from him. "I used to be proud of what you were doing, you know. But it stopped feeling like we were part of your life. It felt like we were props in the story you wanted to tell."

Kincaid's throat tightened. "I thought I was doing this for all of us. For you, for your mom. To make the world better, to leave something behind that mattered."

She leaned forward, her eyes glistening. "And maybe you did, Dad. But sometimes it felt like you left us behind, too."

The room fell silent for a moment, the only sound the faint murmur of aides preparing for the address in the halls below. Finally, Kincaid reached for her hand. "Caroline, I can't change the past. But

I want you to know that you were never a prop to me. You're my daughter, and I've always been proud of you—whether or not I showed it."

Her defenses softened, and she squeezed his hand. "I'm proud of you too, Dad. I just wish it hadn't cost so much."

They sat together for a moment, the tension between them easing into something closer to understanding.

The Farewell Address

The East Room was filled to capacity, the air buzzing with anticipation. Cabinet members, staffers, and foreign dignitaries filled the seats, their faces a mix of solemnity and respect. Cameras were positioned strategically to capture every angle, and beyond the White House, millions of Americans sat in their living rooms, waiting to hear from their outgoing leader one last time.

As Kincaid stepped to the podium, a hush fell over the room. He adjusted the microphone, took a deep breath, and began.

"My fellow Americans, tonight I stand before you for the final time as your President. It has been the honor of my life to serve this country, and as I prepare to pass the torch to a new administration, I want to reflect on where we've been, where we are, and where we are going."

He spoke about the achievements of his administration: expanding healthcare access, the strides made in renewable energy, the diplomatic accords that prevented conflict in volatile regions. But he didn't shy away from the failures either.

"There were moments when we fell short. When I fell short," he admitted, his voice steady but tinged with emotion. "Leadership is not about perfection; it's about striving for progress, even in the face of adversity. I have made mistakes, and I have learned from them. My hope is that we, as a nation, continue to learn and grow together."

Kincaid's tone shifted as he spoke about the challenges ahead. "The world we live in is complex, and the problems we face are daunting. But I believe in the resilience of the American people. I believe in our ability to come together, even when it feels like the divisions are insurmountable. That is the spirit that has carried this nation forward for generations, and it is the spirit that will guide us into the future."

He paused, scanning the room, then added a personal note. "As I prepare to leave this office, I carry with me not just the memories of my time here, but the lessons I've learned from the people I've met—from the factory workers in Michigan to the students in California, from the farmers in Iowa to the entrepreneurs in Georgia. Each of you has reminded me why this country is worth fighting for."

The Aftermath

As Kincaid stepped away from the podium, the room erupted in applause. He glanced at the front row where Caroline sat beside her mother, clapping with tears in her eyes. The moment felt bittersweet—a mix of closure and the weight of goodbye.

Back in the residence, Kincaid watched the replay of the speech with his family. Caroline leaned her head on his shoulder, whispering, "You did good, Dad."

For the first time in months, Kincaid allowed himself to feel a sliver of peace.

10 A NEW DAWN

The crowd stretched endlessly along the National Mall, a sea of faces shrouded in coats and scarves against the January chill. The Capitol stood in stark relief against a crisp, blue sky, its grandeur as timeless as the republic it represented. President David Kincaid stood on the inaugural platform, now as a guest, watching Linda Monroe, his successor, prepare to take the oath of office. The energy in the air was palpable, a mix of optimism and tension—hallmarks of every new administration.

Kincaid's face remained impassive, betraying none of the complicated emotions coursing through him. Around him, dignitaries and political allies exchanged pleasantries, but Kincaid's thoughts were elsewhere. As Chief Justice Fairchild raised her hand to administer the oath, Kincaid's gaze wandered toward the horizon, where the Washington Monument stood resolute.

Reflections on Legacy

The ceremony was a familiar spectacle—stirring music, hopeful speeches, and the inevitable promises of a brighter future. But for Kincaid, it carried a weight that felt uniquely personal. The past eight years had been the most challenging and transformative of his life. He had entered the presidency with a vision: to unite a fractured nation, to lead boldly on issues like climate change, and to restore faith in government. He had accomplished much, but not without missteps.

The scandal that erupted in his final months had shaken his administration, tarnishing his record and leaving an indelible mark on his presidency. Yet, as he stood there watching Monroe, Kincaid felt a sense of closure. His presidency had been imperfect, but it had been honest. The values he fought for—the battles he won and even the ones he lost—were now part of the country's history.

As the crowd erupted in applause at Monroe's inauguration, Kincaid felt a pang of bittersweet pride. He had once stood in her place, brimming with the hope and resolve that came with new beginnings. Now, his role was different. His time in the spotlight was over—for now.

The Final Twist

Later that evening, Kincaid returned to the White House one last time. The historic building felt eerily quiet, emptied of the bustling staff that had defined his presidency. In the Oval Office, Tom Anders awaited him, holding a sealed envelope.

"Tom," Kincaid greeted, his tone curious. "What's this?"

"It's about the leak," Anders replied, his expression grave. "We've uncovered the full story."

Kincaid took the envelope and opened it, his brow furrowing as he scanned the contents. It wasn't just Harrington. The leak had been part of a larger scheme, orchestrated by powerful corporate and political interests. The goal hadn't been merely to derail Kincaid's presidency—it had been to destabilize the transition and weaken Monroe before she even took office.

"Monroe's team knew," Anders continued. "They played along, hoping the fallout would focus solely on your administration. But this runs deeper than either of you."

Kincaid leaned back, the enormity of the revelation sinking in. "So, they wanted chaos. No matter who paid the price."

Anders nodded. "The question is, what do we

do with this?"

Kincaid folded the documents and slid them into his jacket. "We wait. Timing is everything, Tom."

A Private Smile

The next morning, Kincaid walked toward the Capitol steps for the final time, pausing briefly to take in the view. The city was alive with the energy of a new administration, reporters buzzing, aides hustling, and tourists snapping photos. The world was moving on.

But Kincaid wasn't leaving defeated. The revelations about the leak had given him a clarity he hadn't felt in months. There was work to be done—work that didn't require the Resolute Desk or the Oval Office.

As he descended the steps, he caught sight of Caroline waiting by the car, her face warm with encouragement. He glanced back at the Capitol one last time, a faint smile playing on his lips. The smile wasn't for the press or the public. It was a private acknowledgment of what lay ahead—a new chapter, a new fight, and perhaps, one day, a return to the stage he had just left.

The camera shutters clicked as Kincaid walked away, his figure receding into the distance. For now, his presidency was over. But his story was far from finished.

ABOUT THE AUTHOR

Arthur Crandon is a retired lawyer and a prolific writer. He is British and grew up in a rural community in Somerset. Recently, he has been acknowledged as a prominent Political Commentator

He has lived in England, Wales, Hong Kong and the Philippines and now spends most of his time in the Philippines with his Visayan wife and their son.

He loves to hear from anyone who has anything to do with the Philippines – you can email him anytime on:

ac@arthurcrandon.co.uk

If you enjoyed this book, please consider leaving a review – your feedback may help others to discover the book.

If you send me a screenshot of your review, I will send you a copy of another of my Self-Help books.

You can email me on ac@arthurcrandon.co.uk

To leave a review – just go back to the book on Amazon and scroll down – the link to leave a review is on the left hand side.

Thanks, and very best wishes.